Forward

In an era where technological advancements are not just rapid but revolutionary, it becomes imperative for businesses to adapt and evolve. This book, a comprehensive guide to embracing the future, stands as a testament to the transformative power of Augmented Reality (AR) and User Experience (UX) in shaping the business landscapes of tomorrow.

As you delve into these pages, you will embark on a journey through the realms of innovative business strategies and customer engagement models. The case studies presented herein are more than just narratives; they are real-world exemplars of how the integration of AR and UX has rede ned the parameters of customer interaction, satisfaction, and business success.

This book is not just about understanding the technical aspects of AR and UX. It's about envisioning a future where businesses transcend traditional boundaries and venture into new territories of customer engagement and experience.

By adopting these technologies, companies are not merely upgrading their tools; they are revolutionizing their approach towards understanding and fulling human needs.

The forward-looking businesses pro led here have not only adapted to change; they have become the harbingers of change, using AR and UX to create immersive, engaging, and delightful experiences. These experiences do not just meet customer expectations; they exceed them, thereby setting new industry standards.

As you read through each chapter, you will nd insights into how embracing a UX mindset and integrating AR can unlock unprecedented opportunities. This book aims to inspire, inform, and guide business leaders, innovators, and thinkers towards creating a new reality—one that is shaped by foresight, enriched by technology, and anchored in human-centric design.

Welcome to a journey of discovery, where the future of business and technology unfolds in the most enlightening and inspiring ways. Welcome to a new reality of endless possibilities.

UX Mindset

AR, UX, and the Power of Innovation

Chapter 1: Introduction to

AR, UX, and the Power of Innovation

Future-Proofing Business Services

The Need for Futureproofing Business Services

In today's fast-paced and ever-evolving business landscape, it has become increasingly crucial for companies to futureproof their services. The rapid advancements in technology, particularly in the realm of augmented reality (AR), have brought about a paradigm shift in how businesses interact with their customers. As such, adopting a user experience (UX) mindset for AR applications has become imperative for businesses that aim to transform their servicing of products and services.

In order to understand the need for futureproofing business services, it is essential to recognize the transformative power of AR. Augmented reality has the ability to seamlessly merge the physical and digital worlds, creating immersive experiences for users. With the help of AR, businesses can enhance their products and services, offering customers a more engaging and interactive experience.

However, the key to leveraging AR effectively lies in adopting a UX mindset. UX design focuses on creating products and services that are user-centered, intuitive, and provide a seamless experience. When applied to AR applications, this mindset enables businesses to design experiences that not only captivate users but also address their needs and pain points.

Future-proofing business services involves more than just implementing AR technology. It requires a deep understanding of user behavior, preferences, and expectations. By conducting thorough research and analysis, businesses can gain valuable insights into their target audience, enabling them to design AR experiences that align with user expectations.

Additionally, future-proofing business services necessitates staying up to date with the latest trends and advancements in AR technology. This involves continuously monitoring the AR landscape, understanding emerging technologies, and adapting business strategies accordingly. By doing so, businesses can ensure that their AR applications remain relevant and competitive in the dynamic market.

Moreover, future-proofing business services involves fostering a culture of innovation within the organization. This requires encouraging creativity, experimentation, and collaboration among employees. By cultivating an environment that embraces innovation, businesses can stay ahead of the curve and proactively adapt to changing customer needs and market trends.

In conclusion, the need for future-proofing business services in the era of AR and UX is undeniable. By adopting a UX mindset for AR applications, businesses can create immersive and user-centered experiences.

UX Mindset

Future-proofing involves understanding user behavior, staying abreast of technological advancements, and fostering a culture of innovation. By embracing these principles, businesses can transform their servicing of products and services, enhancing customer satisfaction and gaining a competitive edge in the market.

Understanding Augmented Reality (AR) and its Potential

In today's rapidly evolving digital landscape, businesses must constantly adapt to stay ahead of the competition.

AR, UX, and the Power of Innovation

UX Mindset

One emerging technology that has the potential to revolutionize the way businesses interact with their customers is Augmented Reality (AR). In this subchapter, we will explore the concept of AR and its immense potential in transforming the servicing of products and services, particularly by adopting a User Experience (UX) mindset.

At its core, AR blends the physical and digital worlds by overlaying computer-generated content onto real-world environments. This technology has already made significant strides in various industries, from gaming and entertainment to healthcare and retail. By leveraging AR, businesses can enhance customer experiences, streamline operations, and unlock new revenue streams.

One of the key advantages of AR is its ability to provide immersive and interactive experiences. By allowing users to visualize products and services in real-time and realworld contexts, businesses can bridge the gap between physical and online shopping experiences. For example, a furniture company could use AR to enable customers to virtually place and visualize furniture in their own homes before making a purchase decision. This not only enhances customer satisfaction but also reduces returns and boosts sales.

To fully harness the potential of AR, businesses must adopt a UX mindset when developing AR applications. This means prioritizing the user experience throughout the entire design and development process. By understanding user needs, preferences, and pain points, businesses can create AR experiences that are intuitive, engaging, and valuable. This includes optimizing user interfaces, ensuring seamless interactions, and providing relevant and personalized content.

Furthermore, AR presents opportunities for businesses to collect valuable data and insights. By analyzing user interactions within AR environments, businesses can gain a deeper understanding of customer behavior and preferences. This data can be used to re ne marketing strategies, personalize offerings, and improve overall customer satisfaction.

In conclusion, AR has the potential to transform the way businesses service their products and services. By embracing a UX mindset and leveraging the immersive capabilities of AR, businesses can enhance customer experiences, increase efficiency, and drive innovation. As the technology continues to evolve, it is crucial for businesses to stay ahead of the curve and future-proof their services by embracing AR and the power of innovation.

The Role of User Experience (UX) in Business Services

In today's digital age, user experience (UX) plays a crucial role in the success of business services. As businesses continue to transform the way they deliver products and services, understanding the importance of UX becomes paramount. This subchapter explores the signi cance of the UX mindset, particularly in the context of augmented reality (AR) applications, and how it can futureproof business services.

Businesses transforming the servicing of products and services are constantly seeking innovative ways to engage their customers. AR applications have emerged as a powerful tool to enhance customer experiences, providing interactive and immersive experiences like never before. However, the success of these AR applications heavily relies on the UX mindset.

The UX mindset refers to the understanding and prioritization of the user's needs, expectations, and emotions throughout their journey with a particular product or service. In the context of AR applications, the UX mindset ensures that businesses create intuitive and seamless experiences, making it easy for customers to interact with the technology.

By adopting a UX mindset for AR applications, businesses can achieve several benefits. Firstly, it enables them to design and develop AR applications that are user-friendly and accessible to a wide range of customers. This inclusivity is crucial in enhancing customer satisfaction and loyalty.

Secondly, the UX mindset allows businesses to identify pain points and challenges that users may face while using AR applications. By addressing these issues, businesses can improve the overall user experience, resulting in increased customer engagement and retention.

Furthermore, the UX mindset encourages businesses to iterate and continuously improve their AR applications based on user feedback. This iterative process ensures that businesses stay ahead of the competition and deliver exceptional experiences that exceed customer expectations.

In conclusion, the role of user experience (UX) in business services, particularly in the context of augmented reality (AR) applications, cannot be overstated. By adopting a UX mindset, businesses transforming the servicing of products and services can future-proof their offerings. They can create intuitive, user-friendly, and immersive experiences that drive customer satisfaction, engagement, and loyalty. Embracing the UX mindset in the development and delivery of AR applications will empower businesses to stay ahead in this rapidly evolving digital landscape.

Harnessing the Power of Innovation for Business Transformation

In today's rapidly evolving business landscape, the ability to innovate has become a critical factor for success. Organizations that fail to adapt and embrace innovation risk being left behind by their competitors. This subchapter explores the concept of harnessing the power of innovation for business transformation, specifically focusing on the UX mindset for augmented reality (AR) applications.

Businesses across various industries are increasingly recognizing the potential of AR in transforming the way they deliver products and services. AR technology has the capability to enhance user experiences, create immersive environments, and provide realtime information and assistance. However, to truly capitalize on the power of AR, organizations must adopt a UX mindset that places the user at the center of the design process.

UX Mindset

The UX mindset is rooted in the understanding that user experience is not just about aesthetics but encompasses the entire journey of interacting with a product or service. By applying this mindset to AR applications, businesses can ensure that their offerings are user-friendly, intuitive, and provide meaningful value. This, in turn, leads to increased customer satisfaction, loyalty, and ultimately, business growth.

To harness the power of innovation for business transformation, organizations must embrace a culture of creativity and experimentation. This involves fostering an environment that encourages employees to think outside the box and take calculated risks. By empowering employees to explore new ideas and technologies, businesses can unlock innovative solutions that drive competitive advantage.

Furthermore, collaboration and partnerships play a pivotal role in harnessing the power of innovation. By collaborating with external experts, businesses can tap into a wealth of knowledge and experience, accelerating the development and implementation of AR applications. Partnering with technology providers, design agencies, and industry leaders allows organizations to leverage existing expertise and resources, reducing the time and cost of innovation.

In conclusion, the power of innovation is a driving force behind business transformation in the digital age. For organizations looking to future-proof their business services, adopting a UX mindset for AR applications is essential. By placing the user at the center of the design process, fostering a culture of creativity and experimentation, and embracing collaboration and partnerships, businesses can harness the power of innovation to revolutionize the way they deliver products and services. By doing so, they can stay ahead of the curve and remain competitive in an ever-changing market.

Chapter 2: The UX Mindset for Augmented Reality (AR) Applications

Introduction to the UX Mindset

The success of any business in today's digital age is heavily reliant on user experience (UX). As technology continues to advance and reshape the way we interact with products and services, it is crucial for businesses to adopt a UX mindset to stay ahead of the competition. This subchapter titled "Introduction to the UX Mindset" will provide valuable insights into the importance of UX, particularly in the context of augmented reality (AR) applications.

For businesses transforming the servicing of products and services, understanding and embracing the UX mindset is essential. By putting the user at the center of the design process, businesses can create immersive and engaging experiences that build customer loyalty and drive growth. With AR applications becoming increasingly prevalent, it

UX Mindset

is vital for businesses to leverage the power of UX to maximize the potential of this technology.

The UX mindset for AR applications involves designing interfaces and interactions that seamlessly integrate digital content with the real world. By considering the needs, preferences, and limitations of users, businesses can create intuitive and user-friendly AR experiences that enhance customer satisfaction. This subchapter will delve into the principles and methodologies of UX design, highlighting the key considerations and best practices specific to AR applications.

One of the core aspects of the UX mindset is empathy. Businesses need to understand the challenges and goals of their users to develop AR solutions that truly meet their needs. By conducting user research, businesses can gain valuable insights into user behavior, preferences, and pain points, which can then inform the design process. This subchapter will explore various research techniques and methodologies that businesses can employ to gather actionable user insights.

Additionally, this subchapter will delve into the iterative nature of UX design. Businesses must continuously test and re ne their AR applications to ensure optimal user experiences. Through prototyping, user testing, and feedback loops, businesses can identify and address usability issues early on, resulting in a more seamless and enjoyable AR experience for their customers.

In conclusion, the UX mindset is a fundamental aspect of future-proofing business services. By adopting this mindset, businesses can create AR applications that captivate users, drive customer satisfaction, and ultimately, propel their growth. This subchapter will equip businesses transforming the servicing of products and services with the knowledge and tools necessary to embrace the UX mindset for augmented reality applications.

Understanding the Basics of Augmented Reality (AR)

In the fast-paced world of technology and innovation, staying ahead of the competition is crucial for businesses transforming the servicing of products and services. One such transformative technology that has gained significant attention is Augmented Reality (AR). This subchapter aims to provide a comprehensive understanding of the basics of AR, with a specific focus on the UX mindset for AR applications.

Augmented Reality, in simple terms, is a technology that overlays digital information or virtual objects onto the real world, enhancing the user's perception and interaction with their surroundings. Unlike Virtual Reality (VR), which immerses the user in a completely digital environment, AR bridges the gap between the real and virtual worlds, creating an interactive and intuitive user experience.

UX Mindset

For businesses seeking to embrace AR, adopting a UX mindset is crucial. User Experience (UX) encompasses the design, usability, and overall satisfaction a user feels when interacting with a product or service. When it comes to AR applications, businesses must prioritize creating seamless and intuitive experiences that enhance the user's perception of reality.

To create a successful AR application, businesses need to consider several key factors. First and foremost, understanding the target audience and their needs is essential. By empathizing with the end-users, businesses can design AR experiences that align with their expectations and provide value.

Furthermore, designing AR applications that offer a high level of interactivity and customization is essential. Users should have the ability to manipulate virtual objects, gather information, and engage with the AR environment in a way that feels natural and intuitive.

Another crucial aspect is the integration of AR into existing business processes. AR should not be seen as an isolated technology but rather as an enabler to enhance various business functions. By identifying pain points and opportunities within the organization, businesses can leverage AR to streamline processes, improve productivity, and deliver exceptional customer experiences.

Lastly, businesses must prioritize performance and stability. AR applications rely heavily on real-time tracking, 3D rendering, and data processing. Ensuring that the application runs smoothly on a variety of devices and under different conditions is crucial for a seamless user experience.

In conclusion, understanding the basics of Augmented Reality (AR) is paramount for businesses looking to transform the servicing of products and services. By adopting a UX mindset, businesses can design AR applications that not only captivate their audience but also provide tangible value. Implementing AR technology into existing business processes, prioritizing interactivity and customization, and ensuring performance and stability are key considerations for achieving success in the AR realm. With the right approach, businesses can future-proof their services and unlock the power of innovation.

Designing User-Centric AR Experiences

In the fast-paced world of business, staying ahead of the competition requires constant innovation and a forward-thinking mindset. One of the most exciting and promising areas of innovation is augmented reality (AR). As businesses transform the way they service products and services, it is essential to adopt a user-centric approach to designing AR experiences. This subchapter explores the importance of a UX mindset for AR applications and provides insights into creating immersive and impactful user experiences.

UX Mindset

In today's digital age, users expect seamless and intuitive interactions with technology. Augmented reality, with its ability to overlay digital information onto the real world, has the potential to revolutionize how businesses engage with their customers. However, to fully harness the power of AR, it is crucial to prioritize the user experience throughout the design process.

To design user-centric AR experiences, businesses must begin by understanding their target audience. By conducting thorough user research and analysis, businesses can gain insights into user preferences, needs, and pain points. This information can then be used to inform the design decisions, ensuring that the AR experience meets the users' expectations and enhances their overall satisfaction.

Another important aspect of user-centric design is creating intuitive interaction patterns. AR applications should be intuitive and easy to navigate, allowing users to seamlessly interact with the virtual elements in their real-world environment. By leveraging established user interface (UI) and user experience (UX) principles, businesses can create AR experiences that feel natural and intuitive, minimizing the learning curve for users.

Furthermore, businesses must focus on delivering value through their AR experiences. The technology itself is not enough; it is the content and functionality that truly matter. By identifying the specificneeds and pain points of their target audience, businesses can develop AR applications that address these challenges and provide tangible value. Whether it is through product demonstrations, interactive tutorials, or virtual try-on experiences, businesses must strive to enhance the overall user experience and deliver meaningful value to their customers.

Finally, businesses should continuously test and iterate their AR experiences based on user feedback. User testing and feedback sessions can provide valuable insights into areas for improvement, allowing businesses to re ne their AR applications and ensure they meet the evolving needs and expectations of their users.

In conclusion, designing user-centric AR experiences is crucial for businesses transforming the servicing of products and services. By adopting a UX mindset and prioritizing user research, intuitive interaction patterns, value delivery, and continuous iteration, businesses can create immersive and impactful AR experiences that drive customer engagement and satisfaction. Embracing the power of AR and placing users at the center of the design process will future-proof businesses and position them as leaders in their respective industries.

Navigating Challenges in AR User Experience Design

In the rapidly evolving world of technology, businesses are constantly seeking ways to transform their product and service offerings. Augmented Reality (AR) has emerged as a powerful tool that enhances user experiences and provides new opportunities for businesses to engage with their customers. However, designing user experiences in AR presents unique challenges that require a specialized UX mindset.

This subchapter explores the challenges faced by businesses in the realm of AR user experience design and offers insights on how to overcome them. By understanding these challenges, businesses can future-proof their services and stay ahead of the competition.

One of the primary challenges in AR user experience design is the need to seamlessly integrate virtual elements into the real world. Unlike traditional user interfaces, AR interfaces exist in the physical space, requiring careful consideration of the user's surroundings. This subchapter delves into techniques and best practices for designing AR interfaces that blend seamlessly with the real world, enhancing user immersion and interaction.

Another challenge lies in the complexity of AR interactions. AR introduces new forms of input and output that may not be intuitive to users. Designers must carefully consider how users will interact with virtual objects and provide clear instructions to ensure a smooth user experience. This subchapter offers practical tips on designing intuitive AR interactions that are easy for users to understand and navigate.

Furthermore, this subchapter addresses the challenge of balancing information overload in AR experiences. With the ability to overlay digital information onto the real world, there is a risk of overwhelming users with excessive visual clutter. Businesses must carefully curate the information presented in AR interfaces to ensure that it is relevant, contextual, and enhances the user's understanding of the physical environment. Strategies for managing information overload are explored in this subchapter, helping businesses deliver meaningful and engaging AR experiences.

Ultimately, by adopting a UX mindset for AR applications, businesses can unlock the power of innovation and transform their product and service offerings. This subchapter provides valuable insights and practical guidance for businesses looking to navigate the challenges of AR user experience design, ensuring that they future-proof their services and deliver exceptional experiences to their customers.

Conducting User Research and Testing for AR Applications

In order to future-proof your business services and stay ahead in the rapidly evolving world of augmented reality (AR), it is essential to adopt a user experience (UX) mindset when developing AR applications. User research and testing play a vital role in creating successful AR applications that meet the needs and expectations of your target audience.

User research involves understanding the behaviors, motivations, and preferences of your users. By conducting thorough research, you can gain valuable insights into how your audience interacts with AR technology and what they expect from AR applications. This research can be done through various methods such as surveys, interviews, and observational studies. The data collected from user research can help you identify user pain points, preferences, and opportunities for innovation.

Once you have gathered user insights, it is crucial to test your AR applications with real users. User testing allows you to validate your assumptions, identify usability issues, and make necessary improvements. It involves observing users interacting with your AR application and collecting feedback on their experiences. By involving your target audience in the testing process, you can ensure that your AR application meets their needs and provides a seamless user experience.

When conducting user research and testing for AR applications, there are a few key considerations to keep in mind. Firstly, it is important to de ne clear research objectives and testing parameters. This will help you stay focused and gather relevant data. Additionally, it is crucial to recruit a diverse group of participants that represent your target audience. This will ensure that you receive a variety of perspectives and insights.

Furthermore, it is essential to create realistic testing environments that mimic the realworld scenarios in which your AR application will be used. This will help you evaluate its usability and effectiveness in practical situations. It is also important to continuously iterate and improve your AR application based on the feedback and insights gathered from user research and testing.

By adopting a UX mindset and conducting user research and testing for your AR applications, you can ensure that your business services are future-proofed and tailored to the needs of your target audience. This will not only enhance the user experience but also differentiate your business in the competitive AR landscape.

Measuring Success: Key Metrics for AR User Experience

In the fast-paced world of augmented reality (AR) applications, businesses are constantly striving to provide an exceptional user experience (UX) to their customers. As more companies are transforming the servicing of products and services, it has become crucial to adopt a UX mindset for AR applications. This subchapter aims to guide businesses in understanding the key metrics for measuring success in AR user experience.

One of the fundamental metrics for evaluating AR UX is the level of user engagement. This metric measures how effectively the AR application captures and holds the user's attention. It can be assessed by analyzing the average session duration, the frequency of interaction, and the number of repeat users. By tracking these metrics, businesses can gauge the overall appeal and engagement level of their AR application.

Another important metric is user satisfaction. This metric helps businesses understand how satis ed users are with the AR experience. It can be measured through user feedback, ratings, and reviews. Additionally, businesses can conduct surveys to collect quantitative data on user satisfaction. By focusing on improving this metric, companies can ensure that their AR application is meeting the needs and expectations of their target audience.

Furthermore, businesses should also assess the efficiency and effectiveness of their AR application. Metrics such as task completion rate, error rate, and time spent on tasks can provide insights into the usability and functionality of the AR experience. By monitoring these metrics, businesses can identify pain points and areas for improvement, ultimately enhancing the overall user experience.

Lastly, businesses should consider the impact on business goals and outcomes. Metrics such as conversion rates, sales, and customer retention can indicate the success of the AR application in achieving business objectives. By aligning these metrics with specific business goals, companies can ensure that their AR investments are generating a positive return on investment.

In conclusion, measuring the success of AR user experience requires a comprehensive understanding of key metrics. By focusing on user engagement, satisfaction, efficiency, effectiveness, and impact on business goals, businesses can continuously improve their AR applications and future-proof their services. By adopting a UX mindset and leveraging the power of innovation, companies can stay ahead in the ever-evolving world of augmented reality.

Chapter 3: Creating Immersive AR Experiences

Understanding Immersive AR Experiences

In today's rapidly evolving business landscape, it is crucial for companies to stay ahead of the curve and embrace emerging technologies that can enhance their products and services. One such technology that has gained significant traction in recent years is Augmented Reality (AR). AR has the potential to revolutionize the way businesses engage with their customers, providing immersive and interactive experiences that blur the line between the physical and digital worlds.

To fully leverage the power of AR, businesses must adopt a UX mindset for AR applications. User Experience (UX) is the key to creating successful and engaging AR experiences that captivate users and drive business results. By understanding the principles of UX in the context of AR, businesses can create compelling experiences that not only entertain but also deliver value to their customers.

Immersive AR experiences take users on a journey, transporting them to a virtual world where they can interact with digital objects in their physical environment. Whether it's trying on virtual clothes, visualizing furniture in their living room, or exploring new car models in a showroom, AR enables users to experience products and services in a way that was previously unimaginable.

UX Mindset

The success of immersive AR experiences lies in their ability to seamlessly integrate with users' daily lives. By understanding users' needs, preferences, and behaviors, businesses can design AR applications that provide intuitive interactions and a seamless user interface. This requires a deep understanding of human psychology, ergonomics, and design principles that guide the development of AR experiences.

Furthermore, businesses must consider the technical aspects of AR implementation. From device compatibility to real-time tracking and rendering, there are various technical challenges that need to be addressed to ensure a smooth and immersive AR experience. It is essential for businesses to work closely with technology partners and experts who can provide the necessary expertise to overcome these challenges.

By embracing the UX mindset for AR applications, businesses can future-proof their services and products, staying ahead of the competition and delivering exceptional experiences to their customers. Immersive AR experiences have the potential to transform the way businesses operate, enabling them to create unique and personalized interactions that drive customer engagement and loyalty.

In conclusion, understanding immersive AR experiences is crucial for businesses looking to transform their services and products. By adopting a UX mindset and considering both user needs and technical aspects, businesses can create compelling AR applications that captivate users and deliver value. The power of AR lies in its ability to transport users to a virtual world, where they can interact with digital objects in their physical environment. By embracing this technology, businesses can future-proof their services and unlock new opportunities for growth and innovation.

Human-Centered Design Principles for AR

In today's rapidly evolving technological landscape, businesses are constantly looking for innovative ways to transform the servicing of products and services. One such innovation that has gained significant traction is augmented reality (AR), which offers a unique user experience (UX) that can revolutionize how businesses engage with their customers. However, to truly harness the power of AR and create seamless and impactful experiences, it is crucial to adopt a human-centered design approach. This subchapter explores the key principles of human-centered design for AR applications, highlighting the importance of a UX mindset in this emerging eld.

As we navigate through the complexities of integrating Augmented Reality (AR) and User Experience (UX) into business strategies, it is crucial to acknowledge Tesler's Law, or The Law of Conservation of Complexity. This law states that in any system, there exists an inherent amount of complexity that cannot be eradicated. Understanding this principle is vital for businesses venturing into the realm of AR and UX.

Tesler's Law in the Context of AR and UX:

Inherent Complexity: Every process or system has a core level of complexity that is immutable. In the context of AR and UX, this translates to understanding that while these technologies offer revolutionary potential, they also come with their own set of complexities that need careful navigation.

User-Centric Burden Management: The essence of Tesler's Law in AR and UX is to ensure that the burden of complexity is not passed onto the user. Businesses must strive to absorb as much of this inherent complexity during the design and development stages. This approach ensures that the end-user experience is seamless, intuitive, and free from unnecessary complications.

In today's technology-driven market, businesses are in a constant state of evolution, seeking innovative methods to enhance the delivery and servicing of their products. AR emerges as a frontrunner in this quest, offering an unparalleled UX that has the potential to rede ne customer engagement paradigms. However, the key to unlocking the full potential of AR lies in the adoption of a human-centered design approach.

the fundamental principles of human-centered design specifically tailored for AR applications. It underscores the importance of a UX mindset in this burgeoning eld. The focus is on designing AR experiences that are not only technologically advanced but also deeply rooted in understanding and addressing human needs and behaviors.

By balancing the technological intricacies of AR with the principles of human-centered design, businesses can create experiences that are not just innovative but also resonant and meaningful to their users. This approach not only enhances customer engagement but also fosters a sense of loyalty and satisfaction that is crucial in the competitive landscape of today's marketplace.

The first principle of human-centered design for AR is understanding the user. To create meaningful experiences, businesses must have a deep understanding of their target audience, their needs, and their pain points. By conducting user research, businesses can gather insights about their users' preferences, behaviors, and expectations, enabling them to design AR applications that cater to their specificneeds.

The second principle is simplicity. AR applications should be intuitive and easy to use, even for those unfamiliar with the technology. By adopting a minimalist design approach, businesses can ensure that users can quickly grasp the purpose and functionality of the AR application, reducing confusion and enhancing the overall user experience.

Next, personalization is crucial in AR applications. Users should have the ability to customize and tailor their AR experiences to their preferences. By offering options for customization, businesses can create a sense of ownership and empower users to personalize their interactions with the AR application.

Another important principle is context awareness. AR applications should be designed to seamlessly integrate with the users' environment and provide relevant information based on their real-world context. By leveraging location-based services and sensor data, businesses can deliver contextualized content that enhances the users' experience and adds value to their interactions.

Lastly, feedback and iteration are essential in the design process. Businesses should actively seek user feedback and continuously iterate on their AR applications to improve usability and address any pain points. By involving users in the design process, businesses can ensure that their AR applications meet their expectations and deliver a delightful user experience.

In conclusion, the UX mindset for AR applications is crucial for businesses transforming the servicing of products and services. By embracing human-centered design principles, businesses can create AR experiences that are user-friendly, intuitive, personalized, context-aware, and continually improved through feedback and iteration. By adopting these principles, businesses can future-proof their services and stay at the forefront of innovation in the emerging eld of augmented reality.

Designing for Different AR

Platforms and Devices

In today's fast-paced world, businesses are constantly seeking innovative ways to transform the servicing of their products and services. One such avenue that holds tremendous potential is augmented reality (AR). By incorporating AR into their offerings, businesses can enhance the user experience (UX), creating immersive and engaging interactions that leave a lasting impact on their customers. However, designing for different AR platforms and devices requires a specific UX mindset to ensure seamless integration and optimal user satisfaction.

When embarking on the journey of designing for AR, businesses must consider the plethora of platforms and devices available. From smartphones and tablets to smart glasses and headsets, each platform offers unique capabilities and limitations. Understanding these nuances is crucial to delivering a consistent and enjoyable experience across all devices.

The first step in designing for different AR platforms and devices is to adopt an empathetic mindset. Businesses must put themselves in the shoes of their users, understanding their needs, preferences, and limitations. This user-centric approach allows businesses to tailor their AR experiences to meet the expectations and requirements of their target audience.

Next, businesses must familiarize themselves with the technical specifications and capabilities of each platform and device. This knowledge will enable them to leverage the strengths of each platform while mitigating any limitations. For example, designing for smartphones may require optimizing for smaller screens and limited processing power, while designing for smart glasses may involve creating lightweight and non-intrusive visual overlays.

Another important consideration is the user interface (UI) and interaction design. Businesses must ensure that the UI is intuitive and easy to navigate across different devices. This includes designing for gestures, voice commands, and other input methods specific to each platform. Consistency in UI design is also crucial, as users should be able to seamlessly transition between different devices without feeling disoriented.

Furthermore, businesses should prioritize performance optimization to ensure smooth and seamless AR experiences. This involves optimizing for device capabilities, network connectivity, and real-time rendering. By minimizing latency and maximizing responsiveness, businesses can create immersive AR experiences that captivate their audience.

In conclusion, designing for different AR platforms and devices requires a UX mindset that focuses on the user, technical specifications, UI design, and performance optimization. By understanding the unique strengths and limitations of each platform, businesses can future-proof their services and deliver compelling AR experiences. With AR rapidly gaining traction, businesses that embrace this technology and adopt a user centric approach will undoubtedly stand out and thrive in an increasingly competitive landscape.

Incorporating Interactive Elements in AR Experiences

As businesses continue to embrace the potential of augmented reality (AR) applications, it becomes essential to adopt a user experience (UX) mindset in order to create engaging and immersive AR experiences. By incorporating interactive elements into these experiences, businesses can unlock new opportunities for customer engagement, product visualization, and brand storytelling.

One of the key advantages of AR is its ability to bridge the gap between the physical and digital worlds. By overlaying digital content onto the real world, AR can provide users with interactive and dynamic experiences that go beyond static images or videos. This opens up a whole new range of possibilities for businesses to engage with their customers.

One way to incorporate interactive elements in AR experiences is through the use of gesture based interactions. By allowing users to interact with virtual objects using gestures such as swiping, tapping, or pinching, businesses can create a more intuitive and immersive experience. For example, a furniture retailer can enable customers to virtually place and rearrange furniture in their own living spaces, allowing them to visualize how different pieces would look and t before making a purchase.

Another interactive element that can enhance AR experiences is the integration of gamification. By adding game-like elements such as challenges, rewards, or leaderboards, businesses can make AR experiences more entertaining and engaging for users. This can be particularly effective in sectors such as education, training, or marketing, where businesses can leverage gamification to drive user participation and knowledge retention.

Furthermore, businesses can also incorporate interactive storytelling in AR experiences to create memorable and impactful brand experiences. By guiding users through a narrative or interactive journey, businesses can convey their brand message and values in a more compelling and immersive way. This can be done through the use of animated characters, interactive hotspots, or branching narratives, allowing users to actively engage with the brand story.

In conclusion, incorporating interactive elements in AR experiences is crucial for businesses looking to future-proof their services and engage with their customers in new and exciting ways. By adopting a UX mindset and leveraging gesture-based interactions, gamification, and interactive storytelling, businesses can create immersive and engaging AR experiences that leave a lasting impression on their audience. With the power of innovation and AR technology, businesses can transform the way they service their products and services, ultimately driving customer satisfaction, loyalty, and business growth.

Enhancing User Engagement through Gamification in AR

In the rapidly evolving landscape of augmented reality (AR), businesses are constantly seeking innovative ways to engage users and create immersive experiences. One such method that has gained significant traction is gamification – the integration of gaming elements into non-gaming contexts. By leveraging the power of gamification in AR applications, businesses can enhance user engagement and drive customer loyalty like never before.

The UX mindset for augmented reality (AR) applications is crucial in ensuring that users have a seamless and enjoyable experience. With AR, users are able to interact with virtual objects in the real world, blurring the lines between the physical and digital realms. This presents a unique opportunity for businesses to captivate their audience through gamified experiences that leverage the inherent interactivity of AR technology.

By incorporating game mechanics such as points, levels, badges, and leaderboards, businesses can tap into the innate human desire for competition, achievement, and social recognition. For example, a retail company could develop an AR app that allows users to collect virtual items or complete challenges in-store, earning points and rewards along the way. This not only makes the shopping experience more enjoyable but also incentivizes users to explore the store further, increasing the likelihood of making a purchase.

UX Mindset

Another powerful aspect of gamification in AR is the ability to create personalized experiences. By analyzing user data and behavior, businesses can tailor the gamified elements to suit individual preferences and interests. This level of personalization not only enhances user engagement but also fosters a sense of ownership and connection to the brand. Users feel more invested in the experience, leading to increased brand loyalty and advocacy.

Furthermore, gamification in AR can also be utilized as a powerful marketing tool. By incorporating shareable elements such as AR filters or mini-games into their apps, businesses can encourage users to create user-generated content and share it on social media platforms. This not only increases brand visibility but also serves as a form of organic advertising, as users share their experiences with their networks.

In conclusion, the integration of gamification in AR applications holds immense potential for businesses looking to future-proof their services. By leveraging the UX mindset for augmented reality, businesses can enhance user engagement, drive customer loyalty, and create truly immersive experiences. The combination of gamified elements, personalized experiences, and social sharing capabilities can revolutionize the way businesses interact with their customers, ultimately leading to improved brand perception and increased portability.

Chapter 4: AR and UX in Business Services

Transforming Customer Service with AR and UX

In today's rapidly evolving business landscape, customer service has become a critical differentiator for companies seeking to stay ahead of the competition. With the advent of cutting-edge technologies like augmented reality (AR) and the growing importance of user experience (UX), businesses are discovering innovative ways to transform their customer service offerings.

This subchapter explores the intersection of AR and UX, and how these two powerful concepts can revolutionize the way companies serve their customers. For businesses that are in the process of transforming their products and services, adopting a UX mindset for AR applications can be a game-changer.

User experience, or UX, refers to the overall experience that a customer has while interacting with a company's products or services. It encompasses everything from the design and functionality of a website or application to the ease of navigation and the overall satisfaction of the customer. When combined with augmented reality, UX takes on a whole new dimension.

AR technology allows businesses to overlay digital information onto the real world, enhancing the customer experience in ways never before possible. Imagine a customer being able to visualize a product in their own environment before making a purchase, or receiving real-time, step-by-step instructions on how to assemble or use a product. These are just a few examples of how AR can transform customer service.

By adopting a UX mindset for AR applications, businesses can ensure that these experiences are not only visually appealing but also intuitive and user-friendly. This means investing in user research, testing, and iterative design to create seamless and immersive experiences that customers will love.

Furthermore, AR and UX can also be utilized to enhance customer support and troubleshooting. With AR-enabled mobile apps, customers can receive personalized assistance in real-time, eliminating the need for lengthy phone calls or frustrating email exchanges. Whether it's diagnosing a technical issue or providing step-by-step guidance, AR-powered customer service can significantly improve the overall customer experience.

In conclusion, the integration of AR and UX has the potential to transform customer service in profound ways. By adopting a UX mindset for AR applications, businesses can unlock new opportunities to engage and delight their customers, differentiate themselves from competitors, and future-proof their services. As technology continues to evolve, it is crucial for businesses to embrace innovation and leverage the power of AR and UX to create exceptional customer experiences.

Enhancing Sales and Marketing through AR Experiences

In today's rapidly changing business landscape, it has become increasingly evident that businesses need to embrace innovative technologies to stay ahead of the competition. One such technology that is revolutionizing the way businesses interact with their customers is Augmented Reality (AR). In this subchapter, we will explore how businesses can enhance their sales and marketing efforts by incorporating AR experiences into their strategies.

For businesses transforming the servicing of products and services, adopting a UX mindset for AR applications is crucial. User experience (UX) plays a pivotal role in determining the success of any AR experience. By understanding the needs and preferences of their target audience, businesses can create AR experiences that offer seamless interactions and deliver value to their customers.

AR experiences can be a powerful tool in the sales process. By utilizing AR, businesses can provide potential customers with an immersive and interactive experience that goes beyond traditional marketing methods. For example, a furniture retailer can allow customers to visualize how different pieces of furniture would look in their homes through AR apps. This not only enhances customer engagement but also helps in closing sales by removing uncertainties and doubts.

Moreover, AR experiences can also be used to create personalized marketing campaigns. By leveraging data and analytics, businesses can tailor AR experiences to individual customers, providing them with relevant and targeted content. For instance, a clothing retailer can use AR to enable customers to virtually try on different outfits, recommending personalized styles based on their preferences and body type. This level of personalization can significantly improve customer satisfaction and increase conversion rates.

Furthermore, businesses can leverage AR experiences to provide virtual demonstrations and tutorials for their products and services. By allowing customers to interact with virtual models and simulations, businesses can showcase the unique features and benefits of their offerings in a more engaging and memorable way. This not only enhances the customer's understanding but also builds trust and credibility in the brand.

In conclusion, embracing AR experiences can be a game-changer for businesses transforming the servicing of products and services. By adopting a UX mindset and incorporating AR into their sales and marketing strategies, businesses can create immersive and personalized experiences that drive customer engagement, boost sales, and elevate their brand image. As AR technology continues to evolve, businesses must stay proactive and innovative in leveraging its potential to future-proof their services and stay ahead of the competition.

Streamlining Operations with AR and UX

In this subchapter, we delve into the powerful combination of augmented reality (AR) and user experience (UX) and explore how it can revolutionize and future-proof business services. Designed for business owners and professionals who are transforming the servicing of products and services, this subchapter aims to provide valuable insights into adopting a UX mindset for AR applications.

The integration of AR and UX has the potential to streamline operations and enhance the overall customer experience. By leveraging AR technology, businesses can create immersive and interactive experiences that bridge the gap between the physical and digital worlds. This not only improves user engagement but also helps businesses deliver more ef cient and effective services.

One of the key advantages of AR is its ability to overlay digital content onto the real world, providing users with a contextual and personalized experience. By harnessing the power of UX, businesses can ensure that this experience is intuitive, seamless, and enjoyable. Through thoughtful design and user research, businesses can understand their customers' needs and preferences, resulting in AR applications that are user-friendly and easily accessible.

When it comes to streamlining operations, AR and UX can work hand in hand to optimize processes and reduce bottlenecks. For example, AR can be leveraged to provide real-time guidance and instructions to service technicians, enabling them to perform their tasks more efficiently. This not only saves time but also minimizes errors and improves overall productivity.

Moreover, AR can also be used to enhance training programs, allowing employees to learn and practice new skills in a simulated environment. By incorporating UX principles, businesses can create engaging and interactive training modules that facilitate knowledge retention and skill development.

By embracing a UX mindset for AR applications, businesses have the opportunity to differentiate themselves in the market and stay ahead of the competition. By focusing on the user journey and ensuring a seamless and delightful experience, businesses can build stronger customer relationships and drive customer loyalty.

In conclusion, the combination of AR and UX has immense potential for businesses transforming the servicing of products and services. By streamlining operations and enhancing the overall customer experience, businesses can future-proof their services and stay at the forefront of innovation. By adopting a UX mindset, businesses can design AR applications that are intuitive, immersive, and impactful, leading to increased customer satisfaction and business success.

AR and UX in Training and Skill Development

In today's fast-paced business world, staying ahead of the competition requires constant innovation and the ability to transform the way we provide products and services. One of the most promising technologies that have the potential to revolutionize the way we train and develop skills is augmented reality (AR). By combining AR with a user experience (UX) mindset, businesses can create immersive and engaging training experiences that enhance learning outcomes and drive performance improvement.

The UX mindset for AR applications involves designing user interfaces and interactions that are intuitive, seamless, and user-friendly. When applied to training and skill development, this mindset ensures that learners can easily navigate through AR simulations, interact with virtual objects, and access relevant information. By prioritizing user needs and preferences, businesses can create personalized training experiences that cater to different learning styles and preferences.

AR offers unique advantages in training and skill development. By overlaying virtual objects and information onto the real world, AR enables learners to practice and apply their skills in realistic scenarios without the need for physical resources or risking real-world consequences. For example, employees can use AR headsets to simulate complex machinery operations or practice customer interactions in a safe and controlled environment.

UX Mindset

Moreover, AR can provide real-time feedback and guidance to learners, helping them identify areas for improvement and offering personalized coaching. By tracking user interactions and performance metrics, businesses can analyze data and gain valuable insights into the effectiveness of their training programs. This data-driven approach allows for continuous improvement and optimization of training materials and methodologies.

AR and UX in training and skill development also promote collaboration and knowledge sharing. By leveraging AR, remote teams can work together on projects, share their expertise, and learn from each other's experiences. This not only enhances the learning process but also fosters a culture of innovation and continuous learning within the organization.

In conclusion, the combination of AR and a UX mindset has the potential to revolutionize training and skill development in business services. By creating immersive and engaging training experiences, businesses can enhance learning outcomes, drive performance improvement, and future-proof their operations. Embracing this technology and mindset is crucial for businesses looking to transform their servicing of products and services and stay ahead in the ever-evolving business landscape.

Leveraging AR and UX for Product Design and Prototyping

In today's rapidly evolving business landscape, staying ahead of the competition means embracing innovative technologies and incorporating them into your product design and development process. Augmented reality (AR) has emerged as a game-changing technology, offering exciting opportunities for businesses to enhance user experiences and create more immersive and interactive products. However, effectively leveraging AR requires adopting a UX mindset and understanding the unique challenges and considerations involved in designing AR applications.

This subchapter explores the intersection of AR and UX, focusing on how businesses can harness the power of these two disciplines to future-proof their services. By integrating AR into your product design and prototyping process, you can unlock a whole new realm of possibilities and deliver exceptional user experiences.

First and foremost, it is crucial to understand the core principles of UX design and how they apply to AR applications. A UX mindset for AR involves considering the user's context, environment, and interaction patterns to create intuitive and seamless experiences. Whether it's for gaming, retail, or industrial applications, designing AR interfaces requires careful attention to detail, ensuring that information is presented in a way that is both useful and visually appealing.

UX Mindset

Furthermore, this subchapter will delve into the various techniques and tools available for prototyping AR experiences. Prototyping is an essential step in the product development process, enabling businesses to validate their ideas, gather user feedback, and make iterative improvements. With AR, prototyping becomes even more critical as it allows designers to test and re ne the spatial aspects of their applications, ensuring that virtual objects integrate seamlessly into the real world.

Additionally, this subchapter will address the challenges and considerations specific to AR and UX integration. From managing user expectations to optimizing performance and minimizing cognitive load, there are several factors to consider when designing AR experiences. By understanding these challenges and adopting best practices, businesses can create AR applications that not only wow users but also deliver tangible value.

In conclusion, leveraging AR and UX for product design and prototyping is a powerful strategy for future-proofing business services. By embracing the UX mindset for AR applications and understanding the unique considerations involved, businesses can create immersive and intuitive experiences that elevate their products and services to new heights. This subchapter will provide valuable insights and practical tips for businesses looking to harness the power of AR and UX in their quest for innovation and success.

Chapter 5: The Power of Innovation in Future-Proofing Business Services

The Importance of Innovation in Business Transformation

In today's rapidly evolving business landscape, innovation has become a critical driving force behind successful business transformation. As companies strive to stay ahead of the competition and meet the ever-changing needs of their customer's, embracing innovation has become a necessity rather than a choice. This subchapter explores the profound importance of innovation in business transformation, with a specific focus on the UX mindset for augmented reality (AR) applications.

Innovation serves as a catalyst for change, enabling businesses to adapt to emerging technologies and market trends. By fostering a culture of innovation, organizations can unlock new opportunities, streamline processes, and enhance their overall competitiveness. In the context of business transformation, innovation is the key that unlocks the door to success.

When it comes to augmented reality (AR) applications, innovation is vital for transforming the way businesses engage with their customers. The UX mindset, which places the user at the center of the design process, is crucial for creating seamless and engaging AR experiences. By adopting a UX mindset, businesses can ensure that their AR applications are intuitive, user-friendly, and deliver value to their customers.

One of the primary benefits of innovation in business transformation is the ability to gain a competitive edge. By continuously innovating and introducing new products, services, or processes, companies can differentiate themselves from their competitors. This not only attracts new customers but also helps in retaining existing ones, fostering long-term loyalty.

Additionally, innovation contributes to operational efficiency and cost-effectiveness. As businesses embrace innovative technologies and processes, they can streamline their operations, eliminate redundancies, and optimize resource allocation. This not only enhances productivity but also reduces costs, ultimately resulting in improved portability.

Furthermore, innovation enables businesses to stay relevant and future-proof their services. In a rapidly changing world, where technology continues to evolve at an unprecedented pace, companies must adapt to meet the evolving needs of their customers. By embracing innovation, businesses can anticipate market trends and proactively develop solutions that cater to emerging demands.

In conclusion, innovation is a critical component of business transformation, particularly in the context of the UX mindset for augmented reality applications. By adopting a culture of innovation, businesses can gain a competitive edge, improve operational efficiency, and future-proof their services. As technology continues to advance, embracing innovation becomes increasingly crucial for businesses transforming the servicing of products and services. Only by embracing innovation can companies ensure long-term success and sustainable growth in an ever-changing business landscape.

Cultivating a Culture of Innovation

In today's rapidly evolving business landscape, cultivating a culture of innovation is becoming increasingly crucial for organizations seeking to future-proof their services. This subchapter will explore the importance of embracing an innovative mindset, with a specific focus on the user experience (UX) mindset for augmented reality (AR) applications.

Businesses that are transforming the servicing of products and services understand that innovation is not just a buzzword; it is the key to staying ahead of the competition and meeting the ever-changing needs of customers. By fostering a culture of innovation, these organizations create an environment where new ideas are encouraged, collaboration is valued, and experimentation is seen as an essential part of growth.

One of the critical components of cultivating a culture of innovation is adopting a UX mindset for AR applications. Augmented reality has revolutionized the way businesses engage with their customers, allowing for interactive and immersive experiences that bridge the gap between the physical and digital worlds. However, for AR to truly deliver value, it must prioritize the user experience.

A UX mindset involves putting the user at the center of the design process. It requires businesses to empathize with their customers, understand their needs, and create AR applications that not only provide utility but also delight and engage users. By integrating UX principles into the development of AR applications, businesses can ensure that their innovation efforts are not only technologically advanced but also human-centered.

To cultivate a culture of innovation, organizations must encourage creativity and risk-taking. This can be achieved by providing employees with the necessary tools, resources, and support to experiment and explore new ideas. Creating cross-functional teams that bring together individuals with diverse backgrounds and expertise can also foster innovation by encouraging different perspectives and ideas.

Furthermore, organizations need to establish a safe environment where failure is seen as a learning opportunity rather than a setback. By celebrating failures and encouraging employees to learn from them, businesses can create a culture that promotes continuous improvement and iteration.

In conclusion, cultivating a culture of innovation is essential for businesses transforming the servicing of products and services. By adopting a UX mindset for AR applications, organizations can ensure that their innovation efforts are user-centric and provide meaningful experiences. Encouraging creativity, risk-taking, and learning from failures are key elements in fostering a culture of innovation. By embracing these principles, businesses can future-proof themselves and stay ahead in today's ever-changing business landscape.

Identifying and Implementing Innovative AR and UX Strategies

In today's rapidly evolving business landscape, staying ahead of the competition requires a constant focus on innovation. As businesses transform the way they provide products and services, one area that holds immense potential is the integration of augmented reality (AR) applications and user experience (UX) strategies. By adopting a UX mindset for AR, businesses can not only enhance their customer experience but also unlock new opportunities for growth and success.

The first step in identifying innovative AR and UX strategies is to understand the power and potential of these technologies. Augmented reality is a technology that overlays virtual elements onto the real world, creating an immersive and interactive experience. By leveraging AR, businesses can provide customers with enhanced product visualizations, virtual try-ons, and interactive tutorials, among other possibilities. However, the success of AR applications relies heavily on the user experience.

To effectively implement AR and UX strategies, businesses must adopt a UX mindset. This involves understanding the needs and preferences of the target audience and designing AR experiences that seamlessly integrate into their lives. By considering factors such as ease of use, intuitive interactions, and personalization, businesses can create AR applications that provide value and delight to their customers.

Furthermore, businesses must also consider the technical aspects of implementing AR and UX strategies. This includes selecting the right AR platform or software development kit (SDK) and ensuring compatibility with existing systems. Additionally, businesses should invest in training and upskilling their teams to develop the necessary expertise in AR development and UX design.

Implementing innovative AR and UX strategies also requires a comprehensive approach. It involves conducting user research and testing to gather feedback and iterate on the AR experience. Businesses should also consider the scalability and sustainability of their AR applications, ensuring they can adapt to changing technologies and customer expectations.

By embracing AR and UX strategies, businesses can differentiate themselves from competitors and provide exceptional customer experiences. Whether it's through transforming the way products are showcased, providing virtual assistance, or offering immersive brand experiences, AR and UX have the power to revolutionize the way businesses interact with their customers.

In conclusion, identifying and implementing innovative AR and UX strategies is essential for businesses transforming the servicing of products and services. By adopting a UX mindset, businesses can design AR applications that provide value and delight to their customers. However, successful implementation requires a comprehensive approach that considers technical considerations, user feedback, and long-term scalability. By future-proofing their business services with AR and UX, businesses can stay ahead in today's dynamic and ever-changing market.

Overcoming Barriers to Innovation in Business Services

In today's rapidly evolving business landscape, innovation is no longer a luxury but a necessity for businesses looking to stay ahead of the competition. This is especially true in the realm of business services, where the ability to transform the way products and services are delivered can make all the difference. However, despite the numerous benefits that innovation brings, there are often barriers that hinder its implementation. In this subchapter, we will explore some of the common barriers to innovation in business services and discuss strategies to overcome them.

One of the major barriers to innovation in business services is the resistance to change. Many businesses are comfortable with the status quo and reluctant to embrace new technologies or approaches. This resistance often stems from a fear of the unknown and a lack of understanding of the potential benefits. To overcome this barrier, businesses must foster a culture of innovation, where employees are encouraged to think creatively and take calculated risks. This can be achieved through training programs, workshops, and creating a safe space for experimentation.

Another barrier to innovation in business services is the lack of a UX mindset for augmented reality (AR) applications. AR has the potential to revolutionize the way businesses deliver services, providing immersive and interactive experiences for customers. However, without a proper understanding of user experience (UX) principles, businesses may struggle to effectively leverage AR technology. To overcome this barrier, it is crucial for businesses to invest in UX research and design, ensuring that AR applications are intuitive, user-friendly, and provide real value to customers.

Furthermore, a lack of financial resources can also hinder innovation in business services. Implementing new technologies and processes often requires a significant investment, which may not be feasible for all businesses, especially smaller ones. To overcome this barrier, businesses can explore alternative funding options such as grants, partnerships, or seeking venture capital. Additionally, adopting a phased approach to innovation, starting with smaller, more manageable projects, can help mitigate financial risks and build a case for further investment.

In conclusion, innovation is essential for businesses transforming the servicing of products and services in the realm of business services. By addressing barriers such as resistance to change, lack of UX mindset for AR applications, and limited financial resources, businesses can unlock the full potential of innovation. Embracing a culture of innovation, investing in UX research and design, and exploring alternative funding options are all crucial steps towards future-proofing business services. By doing so, businesses can not only stay ahead of the competition but also provide enhanced experiences and value to their customers.

Measuring the Impact of Innovation on Business Performance

In today's rapidly evolving business landscape, innovation has become a key driver of success. As businesses transform the way they deliver products and services, it becomes essential to measure the impact of innovation on business performance. This subchapter explores the various metrics and methodologies used to evaluate the effectiveness of innovation initiatives, with a specific focus on the UX mindset for augmented reality (AR) applications.

One of the primary metrics used to measure the impact of innovation is the return on investment (ROI). This metric helps businesses determine the financial benefits derived from their innovation efforts. By quantifying the costs associated with innovation and comparing them to the resulting revenue or cost savings, businesses can assess whether their innovation initiatives are yielding positive returns.

UX Mindset

However, measuring the impact of innovation goes beyond financial metrics. Businesses also need to consider the impact on customer satisfaction, brand loyalty, and market share. This is where the UX mindset comes into play. User experience (UX) is a critical factor in the success of AR applications, as it directly influences customer engagement and satisfaction. Therefore, businesses must measure the impact of their AR applications on user experience and customer satisfaction.

To measure the impact of AR applications on user experience, businesses can employ various techniques. Usability testing allows businesses to gather feedback from users and assess the effectiveness of their AR applications in meeting user needs and expectations. User surveys and feedback mechanisms can provide valuable insights into the satisfaction levels of users and help identify areas for improvement.

In addition to UX metrics, businesses should also consider the impact of AR applications on key performance indicators (KPIs) such as conversion rates, average order value, and customer retention. By analyzing these KPIs before and after the implementation of AR applications, businesses can evaluate the impact of innovation on business performance.

Measuring the impact of innovation on business performance is a complex task that requires a comprehensive approach. By considering both financial metrics and UX mindset for AR applications, businesses can gain a holistic understanding of the effectiveness of their innovation initiatives. This knowledge will enable them to make informed decisions and continuously improve their products and services to meet the evolving needs of their customers.

Chapter 6: Future Trends and Challenges in AR, UX, and Business Services

Emerging Trends in AR and UX

As businesses continue to evolve in the digital age, the integration of augmented reality (AR) and user experience (UX) has become increasingly vital. This subchapter explores the emerging trends in AR and UX and highlights the importance of adopting a UX mindset for AR applications.

AR technology has gained significant traction in recent years, allowing users to interact with the digital world in a more immersive and realistic way. From gaming and entertainment to retail and healthcare, AR has the potential to revolutionize various industries. However, to fully harness the power of AR, businesses must prioritize the user experience.

A UX mindset for AR applications involves putting the user at the center of the design process. It is crucial to understand the needs, preferences, and behaviors of users to create seamless and intuitive AR experiences. By adopting a UX mindset, businesses can ensure that AR applications deliver value, engage users, and enhance their overall experience.

One emerging trend in AR and UX is the integration of artificial intelligence (AI) and machine learning (ML) algorithms. These technologies enable AR applications to adapt and personalize the user experience based on individual preferences and behaviors. By analyzing user data and patterns, AI and ML algorithms can provide personalized recommendations, improve usability, and enhance the overall AR experience.

Another trend is the integration of AR into ecommerce and retail experiences. With AR, customers can virtually try on clothes, visualize furniture in their homes, or even test drive cars. By integrating AR into the shopping experience, businesses can provide customers with a more immersive and interactive way to explore products, leading to increased engagement, conversion rates, and customer satisfaction.

Furthermore, the use of AR in training and education is another emerging trend. AR can enhance learning experiences by providing interactive and immersive content. For instance, medical students can use AR to practice surgical procedures in a simulated environment, while employees can receive real-time guidance and instructions through AR overlays. By leveraging AR in training and education, businesses can improve knowledge retention, skills development, and overall performance.

In conclusion, the emerging trends in AR and UX are transforming the way businesses deliver products and services. By adopting a UX mindset for AR applications, businesses can create immersive, personalized, and engaging experiences for their users. Integrating AI and ML algorithms, incorporating AR into e-commerce, and leveraging AR for training and education are just a few examples of the exciting possibilities that lie ahead. Embracing these trends will future-proof business services, enabling them to stay ahead of the curve and meet the evolving needs of their customers.

Anticipating Challenges in Implementing AR and UX Strategies

In today's rapidly evolving business landscape, organizations are constantly seeking innovative ways to enhance their products and services. One of the most promising avenues for achieving this is through the integration of augmented reality (AR) and user experience (UX) strategies. However, implementing AR and UX solutions is not without its challenges. In this subchapter, we will explore some of the key obstacles that businesses may face when adopting AR and UX technologies and strategies and offer insights on how to overcome them. One of the primary challenges in implementing AR and UX strategies is the need for a UX mindset specifically tailored for AR applications. While UX principles and practices are well-established in traditional digital environments, AR presents unique design considerations. User interaction in AR involves the physical world, and designers must carefully consider how to seamlessly blend digital content with the user's physical surroundings. This requires a deep understanding of how users perceive and interact with AR interfaces, as well as the ability to create intuitive and immersive experiences. Businesses must invest in training their design teams to think in terms of AR-specific UX principles to ensure successful implementation.

Another challenge lies in the technical complexities associated with AR. AR applications require advanced computer
vision, tracking, and rendering technologies, all of which demand significant computational power and expertise. Businesses must have the infrastructure in place to support these requirements, which may involve upgrading hardware, investing in cloud services, or collaborating with technology partners. Additionally, ensuring compatibility across different devices and platforms can be a daunting task. It is crucial for businesses to conduct thorough testing and quality assurance processes to deliver a consistent and seamless AR experience to users.

Furthermore, privacy and security concerns are another hurdle to overcome. AR applications often collect and process vast amounts of user data, including location information and personal preferences. Businesses must prioritize data protection and ensure that robust security measures are in place to safeguard user privacy. Transparency in data collection and usage is essential to build trust with users and maintain a positive brand reputation.

In conclusion, while the integration of AR and UX strategies offers immense potential for transforming business services, it is not without its challenges. To successfully implement AR and UX technologies, businesses must cultivate a UX mindset specifically tailored for AR applications, address technical complexities, and prioritize user privacy and data security. By anticipating and proactively addressing these challenges, businesses can future-proof their services and unlock new opportunities for innovation and growth in the digital age.

Exploring Ethical Considerations in AR and UX

In today's rapidly evolving technological landscape, businesses are increasingly adopting augmented reality (AR) applications to enhance their products and services. As companies strive to provide immersive and engaging user experiences (UX), it is crucial to address the ethical considerations associated with AR and UX. This subchapter delves into the importance of developing a UX mindset for AR applications while navigating the ethical challenges that arise.

Understanding the UX mindset for AR applications is vital for businesses transforming the servicing of products and services. AR technology has the potential to revolutionize the way customers interact with brands, offering unique and personalized experiences. However, this transformation must be approached with a strong focus on user centered design and the ethical implications that accompany it.

One of the key ethical considerations in AR and UX is privacy. AR applications often rely on capturing and analyzing user data to deliver customized experiences. Businesses must ensure that user data is collected and used responsibly, with clear consent and transparency. Respecting user privacy builds trust and fosters long-term relationships with customers.

Another ethical consideration is the potential for addiction and overuse. AR experiences can be highly immersive, captivating users for extended periods. Businesses must strike a balance between providing engaging experiences and encouraging healthy usage habits. Designing AR applications with features that promote breaks, limit screen time, and prioritize user well-being is essential.

Furthermore, ethical considerations also extend to the content and messaging within AR experiences. Businesses should be cautious about promoting harmful or discriminatory content through their applications. It is crucial to consider the potential impact of AR experiences on diverse user groups and ensure that the content aligns with inclusive and ethical values.

Additionally, businesses must address the potential for misinformation and manipulation within AR experiences. As augmented reality blurs the line between the real and virtual worlds, there is an increased risk of spreading false information or distorting reality. Companies should prioritize accuracy, factchecking, and responsible content curation to maintain trust and integrity.

By proactively exploring and addressing these ethical considerations, businesses can futureproof their AR and UX strategies. Embracing a UX mindset that prioritizes user needs, privacy, inclusivity, and responsible content creation will not only enhance customer satisfaction but also protect the brand's reputation.

In conclusion, as businesses transform the servicing of products and services through AR applications, it is essential to consider the ethical implications of these technologies. Developing a UX mindset that prioritizes privacy, user well-being, inclusivity, and responsible content creation is crucial. By incorporating these considerations into their AR and UX strategies, businesses can futureproof their services and build strong and ethical relationships with their customers.

The Future of Business Services in the Era of AR and UX

In today's rapidly evolving digital landscape, businesses are constantly seeking innovative ways to transform the servicing of their products and services. One of the most promising technologies that has the potential to revolutionize the way businesses interact with their customers is augmented reality (AR). By integrating AR with an enhanced user experience (UX) mindset, businesses can create immersive, interactive, and personalized experiences for their customers, ultimately driving growth and success in the marketplace.

AR, a technology that overlays digital information onto the real world, has already made significant inroads in various industries. From gaming and entertainment to healthcare and manufacturing, AR has proven to be a game-changer, enabling businesses to enhance their operations and deliver unique value propositions. However, to truly harness the power of AR, businesses must adopt a UX mindset that places the user at the center of their design and development processes.

The UX mindset for AR applications requires businesses to prioritize user needs, emotions, and behaviors throughout the entire customer journey. By understanding how users interact with AR experiences, businesses can create intuitive interfaces, seamless interactions, and memorable moments that capture the attention and loyalty of their customers. Moreover, the UX mindset also emphasizes the importance of continuous iteration and improvement, ensuring that businesses stay ahead of the curve and adapt to changing customer preferences and technological advancements.

In the future, the convergence of AR and UX will have profound implications for business services. From retail and e-commerce to hospitality and education, businesses will be able to leverage AR and UX to transform the way they engage with customers. Imagine a virtual showroom where customers can try on clothes and accessories without physically being present or a personalized digital assistant that guides users through complex tasks with ease. These scenarios are just the tip of the iceberg when it comes to the possibilities that AR and UX can unlock for business services.

However, embracing AR and UX requires businesses to invest in the right talent, infrastructure, and mindset. Companies need to hire professionals with expertise in AR development, UX design, and data analytics to create compelling experiences that resonate with users. They also need to invest in robust AR hardware and software solutions to deliver seamless and immersive experiences. Additionally, businesses must foster a culture of innovation and experimentation, encouraging employees to think outside the box and push the boundaries of what is possible with AR and UX.

In conclusion, the future of business services lies in the synergistic integration of AR and UX. By adopting a UX mindset for AR applications, businesses can create transformative experiences that delight customers and drive business growth. However, to future-proof their services, businesses must embrace innovation, invest in the right talent and infrastructure, and foster a culture of experimentation. The era of AR and UX is here, and businesses that seize the opportunities it presents will be the ones that thrive in the digital age.

Conclusion: Empowering Business Transformation through AR, UX, and Innovation

In today's rapidly evolving business landscape, the successful transformation of products and services is paramount to staying ahead of the competition. This subchapter explores the synergistic relationship between augmented reality (AR), user experience (UX), and innovation in empowering businesses to future-proof their services.

For businesses transforming the servicing of products and services, adopting a UX mindset for AR applications is crucial. AR has the potential to revolutionize the way businesses interact with their customers, providing immersive and interactive experiences.
However, it is essential to prioritize user experience to ensure that these applications deliver real value and engage customers effectively.

AR applications can enhance customer experiences by providing virtual product demonstrations, interactive manuals, and personalized recommendations. By leveraging the power of AR, businesses can create memorable and engaging experiences that not only satisfy customers but also drive brand loyalty and increase sales.

UX Mindset

To achieve this, businesses must embrace innovation, constantly exploring new ways to leverage AR technology and enhance user experiences. Innovation is not limited to the development of cutting-edge AR applications but also extends to the integration of AR into existing business processes and work ows. By thinking creatively and embracing a culture of innovation, businesses can uncover new opportunities to leverage AR and transform their services.

However, it is crucial to understand that AR and UX alone are not enough to future-proof business services. Innovation must be the driving force behind the adoption of AR and UX. By fostering a culture of innovation, businesses can continuously adapt to changing market dynamics and customer expectations. This includes embracing emerging technologies, experimenting with new business models, and actively seeking customer feedback.

Future-proofing business services requires a holistic approach that combines AR, UX, and innovation. By integrating these three elements, businesses can create exceptional customer experiences that set them apart from the competition. Embracing a UX mindset for AR applications and fostering a culture of innovation will enable businesses to stay ahead of the curve and thrive in an everchanging business landscape.

In conclusion, the future of business services lies in the seamless integration of AR, UX, and innovation. This subchapter has explored the importance of adopting a UX mindset for AR applications and the transformative power of innovation. By harnessing these elements, businesses can empower their transformation efforts and create services that are futureproof and customer-centric.

Appendix A: Glossary of Key Terms

In the rapidly evolving world of business services, staying ahead of the curve requires a deep understanding of the key terms and concepts that drive innovation. This glossary aims to provide a comprehensive overview of the essential terminology related to the UX mindset for augmented reality (AR) applications. Whether you are a business transforming the servicing of products and services or an individual seeking to futureproof your career, this glossary will serve as a valuable resource.

1.   Augmented Reality (AR): A technology that overlays digital information, such as images, videos, or sounds, onto the real-world environment, enhancing the user's perception and interaction with their surroundings.

2.   User Experience (UX): The overall experience a person has when interacting with a product or service, encompassing their emotions, attitudes, and opinions. UX design focuses on creating seamless and enjoyable experiences for users.

3.   UX Mindset: A way of thinking that prioritizes the user's needs, desires, and limitations, placing them at the

center of the design process. A UX mindset encourages empathy, usability, and continuous improvement.

4.   Immersion: The degree to which a user feels fully engaged and absorbed in an augmented reality experience. Immersive AR applications often provide a sense of presence and realism, blurring the boundaries between the digital and physical worlds.

5.   Interaction Design: The practice of designing the ways in which users engage with digital interfaces. It involves creating intuitive and meaningful interactions that enable users to achieve their goals effectively.

6.   Haptic Feedback: The use of tactile sensations, such as vibrations or touch, to provide users with physical feedback during AR interactions. Haptic feedback enhances the sense of realism and improves the user's understanding of the virtual objects.

7.   Computer Vision: A field of artificial intelligence that enables computers to understand and interpret visual information from the real world. Computer vision is crucial in AR applications for object recognition, tracking, and scene understanding.

8.   Spatial Computing: The ability of computers to understand and interact with the physical space around them. Spatial computing is essential for AR applications as it allows virtual objects to be anchored and interact with the real world accurately.

9.   Marker less Tracking: A technique used in AR to track the position and orientation of an object or user without the need for physical markers or sensors. Marker less tracking relies on computer vision algorithms and sensor data to provide seamless AR experiences.

10.   Usability Testing: A method used to evaluate the effectiveness, efficiency, and satisfaction of a product or service by observing real users performing specific tasks. Usability testing helps identify and address usability issues to improve the overall user experience.

11.   Complexity Transfer: The concept of shifting complexity from one area of a system to another. In the context of Tesler's Law, this often involves moving complexity from the user interface to the back end, or vice versa, to achieve an optimal user experience.

12.   System Design: The process of defining the architecture, components, and interfaces of a system to satisfy specified requirements. Effective system design in the context of Tesler's Law involves balancing complexity between the user interface and the system's functionality.

13.   Simplicity: The quality of being easy to understand or use. In the context of Tesler's Law, simplicity refers to the goal of making user interfaces as straightforward as possible, despite the inherent complexity of the system.

14.   Inherent Complexity: The essential complexity that is a fundamental part of a system's nature. It cannot

be eliminated but can be managed through intelligent design and user experience considerations.

15.   Back End: The part of a system that operates behind the scenes, handling the core functionality and processing. The back end is typically where a significant portion of a system's complexity is managed and resolved.

16.   Complexity: The degree of intricacy, complication, or sophistication within a system. In the context of Tesler's Law, it refers to the inherent challenges or difficulties involved in designing and using a system.

17.   Tesler's Law: Also known as The Law of Conservation of Complexity, it posits that every system has an inherent level of complexity that cannot be reduced or removed. Instead, this complexity must be managed and distributed between the user interface and the system's back end.

By familiarizing yourself with these key terms, you are equipped with the foundational knowledge needed to embrace the UX mindset for augmented reality applications. As you navigate the world of business services and seek to future-proof your organization, understanding these concepts will enable you to harness the power of innovation and create remarkable user experiences.

Appendix B:

Recommended Resources for Further Reading

As businesses continue to embrace the power of innovation and explore new ways to transform the servicing of products and services, it is crucial to stay updated with the latest trends and best practices. This appendix provides a curated list of recommended resources for further reading, specifically tailored to those interested in developing a UX mindset for augmented reality (AR) applications.

1. "The Fourth Transformation: How Augmented Reality & Artificial Intelligence Will Change Everything" by Robert Scoble and Shel Israel - This book offers valuable insights into the future of AR and its potential impact on businesses. It explores the intersection of AR, AI, and other emerging technologies, providing a roadmap for organizations looking to future-proof their services.

2. "Designing for Mixed Reality: A Practical Guide to Creating AR/VR Experiences" by Valerie Vacante - This comprehensive guidebook helps businesses understand the principles and techniques involved in designing compelling AR experiences. It covers topics such as user-centered design, interaction patterns, and prototyping, allowing readers to develop a solid foundation in creating user-friendly AR applications.

3. "Augmented Human: How Technology is Shaping the New Reality" by Helen

Papagiannis - In this thought-provoking book, Papagiannis delves into the ways in which augmented reality is transforming human experiences. It offers practical insights into designing AR interfaces, understanding user behavior, and leveraging AR to enhance business services.

4. "Virtual, Augmented, and Mixed Realities in Education" edited by Michael Thomas and Eunice Ivala - This collection of research papers explores the educational implications of AR and other immersive technologies. By examining case studies and theoretical frameworks, it provides valuable insights into how businesses can leverage AR to improve their training and educational services.

5. "Augmented Reality Law, Privacy, and Ethics: Law, Society, and Emerging AR Technologies" by Brian Wassom - As businesses navigate the legal and ethical considerations surrounding AR applications, this book offers a comprehensive overview of the legal landscape. It covers topics such as intellectual property, privacy, and data protection, ensuring that businesses can develop AR solutions while staying compliant with applicable laws.

6. "Augmented Human: How Technology Is Shaping the New Reality" by Helen Papagiannis - Augmented Reality (AR) blurs the boundary between the physical and digital worlds. In AR's current exploration phase, innovators are beginning to create compelling and contextually rich applications that enhance a user's everyday experiences. In this book, Dr. Helen Papagiannis—a world leading expert in the

eld—introduces you to AR: how it's evolving, where the opportunities are, and where it's headed.

These resources provide a wealth of knowledge and insights for businesses looking to embrace the UX mindset for AR applications. By delving into the recommended reading materials, businesses can gain a deeper understanding of the potential of AR, its design principles, legal considerations, and its impact on education. Armed with this knowledge, organizations can future-proof their services and leverage the power of innovation to stay ahead in today's rapidly evolving business landscape.

Appendix C: Case Studies on Successful AR and UX Implementation

Let's delve into several case studies that highlight the successful implementation of augmented reality (AR) and user experience (UX) in various industries. These case studies serve as practical examples for businesses transforming the servicing of products and services, showcasing the power of innovation and the UX mindset for AR applications.

1.   Retail: One of the most prominent examples of successful AR implementation in the retail industry is IKEA's AR app. By utilizing AR technology, IKEA allows customers to virtually place furniture and decor in their own homes before making a purchase. This

immersive experience enhances customer engagement, increases confidence in purchasing decisions, and reduces returns, ultimately boosting sales and customer satisfaction.

2.   Healthcare: In the healthcare sector, AR and UX have been leveraged to improve patient outcomes. For instance, AccuVein, a medical device company, developed a handheld device using AR technology to help healthcare professionals locate veins for blood draws and IV insertions. This AR solution reduces patient discomfort, minimizes the risk of complications, and enhances overall efficiency in healthcare settings.

3.   Manufacturing: AR and UX have also revolutionized the manufacturing industry. Toyota, for instance, implemented AR glasses for their assembly line workers. These glasses provide real-time instructions and visualizations, guiding workers through complex assembly processes and reducing errors. This innovative use of AR technology has significantly improved productivity and quality control in Toyota's manufacturing operations.

4.   Tourism: AR and UX have transformed the tourism industry by providing immersive experiences for travelers. The Louvre Museum in Paris, for example, offers an AR-guided tour that enhances visitors' exploration of the museum's exhibits. By overlaying digital information onto the real-world environment, visitors gain deeper insights into the artworks, enhancing their overall museum experience.

These case studies demonstrate the transformative potential of AR and UX in various industries. By adopting a UX mindset for AR applications, businesses can create immersive and engaging experiences that drive customer satisfaction, improve operational efficiency, and boost revenue. However, successful implementation requires careful consideration of user needs, seamless integration of AR technology, and continuous evaluation and refinement of the user experience.

In conclusion, the case studies presented in this subchapter provide real-world examples of how businesses have future-proofed their services through the successful implementation of AR and UX. By embracing these technologies and adopting a UX mindset, businesses can unlock new opportunities, enhance customer experiences, and gain a competitive edge in today's rapidly evolving marketplace.

Appendix D: Tools and Technologies for AR and UX Development

As businesses continue to embrace the power of innovation, augmented reality (AR) and user experience (UX) development are becoming essential components of their digital transformation strategies. In this subchapter, we will explore the tools and technologies that are crucial for businesses looking to adopt a UX mindset for AR applications.

1. AR Frameworks and Platforms: AR frameworks and platforms provide the foundation for developing immersive AR experiences. Examples include ARKit and ARCore, which enable developers to create AR applications for iOS and Android devices respectively. These frameworks offer features such as motion tracking, object recognition, and light estimation, allowing for the seamless integration of virtual objects into the real world.

2. 3D Modeling and Design Tools: To create realistic and engaging AR experiences, businesses need access to 3D modeling and design tools. Tools such as Blender, Autodesk Maya, and SketchUp allow designers to create and manipulate 3D models of objects, environments, and characters. These models can then be imported into AR development platforms for further refinement and integration.

3. UX Design Tools:
UX design plays a crucial role in ensuring that AR applications are intuitive, user-friendly, and enjoyable. Tools like Sketch, Adobe XD, and Figma enable designers to create wireframes, prototypes, and interactive mockups of AR interfaces. These tools facilitate collaboration between designers and developers, ensuring a seamless user experience throughout the AR application.

4. Computer Vision Libraries:

UX Mindset

Computer vision libraries, such as OpenCV and TensorFlow, are essential for AR applications that involve object recognition, tracking, and gesture recognition. These libraries provide developers with pre-trained models and APIs that simplify the implementation of computer vision algorithms. By leveraging these tools, businesses can create AR experiences that seamlessly interact with the real world.

5. Cloud Services:
Cloud services play a vital role in AR and UX development by providing scalable and reliable infrastructure for hosting AR content and delivering it to users. Services like Amazon Web Services (AWS) and Microsoft Azure offer features such as content delivery networks (CDNs), serverless computing, and machine learning capabilities. These services enable businesses to deliver high-quality AR experiences without worrying about infrastructure limitations.

By leveraging these tools and technologies, businesses can future-proof their services and enhance their customer experiences through AR applications. Adopting a UX mindset for AR development ensures that these applications are intuitive, immersive, and aligned with the needs and expectations of their target audience. Embracing these tools will allow businesses to stay ahead in the rapidly evolving digital landscape and drive innovation in their respective niches.

As we reach the culmination of "UX Mindset: Exploring Digital-to-Physical Interactions," it is evident that the journey through the landscape of user experience (UX) is as evolving as it is enlightening. This book has traversed various facets of UX, emphasizing the seamless integration of digital and physical realms to enhance user interactions and experiences.

it's clear that the journey into the world of Augmented Reality (AR) and User Experience (UX) is not just a passage through emerging technologies, but a deep dive into the future of business innovation. This book has navigated the intersection of AR and UX, underlining the crucial role they play in transforming and future-proofing business services.

From the outset, we examined the core principles of UX, recognizing its critical importance in the integration of digital and physical interactions. The exploration of AR brought to life the immense possibilities that lie in enhancing user experiences, transcending traditional boundaries, and offering immersive, engaging customer interactions.

Key to this discussion has been the understanding of Tesler's Law and its implications in designing user-centric services. Balancing inherent complexity with user simplicity, the book highlighted the necessity of a user-first approach, ensuring that the sophistication of technology enhances rather than complicates the user experience.

As the book progressed, we delved into case studies and practical applications, showcasing real-world examples of businesses that have successfully harnessed the power of

UX Mindset

AR and UX. These narratives served not just as illustrations but as blueprints for adopting a forward-thinking, innovative mindset.

The future of business services, as we've seen, is intrinsically linked to the evolution of technology. But more importantly, it's about how these technological advancements are harnessed to create value for users. The 'UX Mindset' has emerged as a fundamental philosophy in this regard, prioritizing user needs and experiences in the design and implementation of technological solutions.

In closing, "Future-proofing Business Services: AR, UX, and the Power of Innovation" is a call to action for businesses and innovators. It encourages a proactive embrace of emerging technologies, not as an end in themselves, but as tools for creating more meaningful, efficient, and engaging user experiences. As we look to the future, the principles and insights shared in this book will serve as guiding lights in the ongoing journey of business innovation, ensuring that services remain relevant, user centric, and ahead of the curve in a rapidly evolving digital landscape.

UX Mindset

Future-proofing Business Services: AR, UX, and the Power of Innovation

I am thrilled to share my journey and dedication to exploring the dynamic realm of spatial reality and the fascinating study of digital-to-physical interactions. In our fast-paced and ever-

evolving business landscape, the urgency to future-proof services has never been more critical.

The rapid advancements in technology, especially in the realm of augmented reality (AR), have ushered in a revolutionary change in the way businesses interact with their customers.

This evolution is not just a technological leap; it represents a paradigm shift in customer engagement and experience. My focus lies at the heart of this transformation – adopting a user experience (UX) mindset in the application of AR technologies. This approach is imperative for businesses that aspire to innovate and transform their servicing of products and services.

Through my work, I aim to bridge the gap between the digital and physical worlds, creating immersive, intuitive, and impactful experiences that resonate with users on a deeper level.

Joshua Carlson